You, Me and Mrs Jones

A Play for Youth Groups

Tony Horitz

A Samuel French Acting Edition

SAMUELFRENCH-LONDON.CO.UK
SAMUELFRENCH.COM

Copyright © 1987 by Samuel French Ltd
All Rights Reserved

YOU, ME AND MRS JONES is fully protected under the copyright laws of the British Commonwealth, including Canada, the United States of America, and all other countries of the Copyright Union. All rights, including professional and amateur stage productions, recitation, lecturing, public reading, motion picture, radio broadcasting, television and the rights of translation into foreign languages are strictly reserved.

ISBN 978-0-573-12272-9

www.samuelfrench-london.co.uk

www.samuelfrench.com

For Amateur Production Enquiries

United Kingdom and World excluding North America

plays@SamuelFrench-London.co.uk

020 7255 4302/01

Each title is subject to availability from Samuel French, depending upon country of performance.

CAUTION: Professional and amateur producers are hereby warned that YOU, ME AND MRS JONES is subject to a licensing fee. Publication of this play does not imply availability for performance. Both amateurs and professionals considering a production are strongly advised to apply to the appropriate agent before starting rehearsals, advertising, or booking a theatre. A licensing fee must be paid whether the title is presented for charity or gain and whether or not admission is charged.

The professional rights in this play are controlled by Samuel French Ltd, 52 Fitzroy Street, London, W1T 5JR.

No one shall make any changes in this title for the purpose of production. No part of this book may be reproduced, stored in a retrieval system, or transmitted in any form, by any means, now known or yet to be invented, including mechanical, electronic, photocopying, recording, videotaping, or otherwise, without the prior written permission of the publisher. No one shall upload this title, or part of this title, to any social media websites.

The right of Tony Horitz to be identified as author of this work has been asserted by him in accordance with Section 77 of the Copyright, Designs and Patents Act 1988

CHARACTERS

Jack
Nobody/Somebody
No one/Some one
Zap
Pow } members of Lenny's gang
Crunch
Lenny
Lena
McConnemmall } members of The Booties
Leader
Booties
Three pop fans
Bouncer
Other fans whole Company
The Electric Crusader
Thunder Woman
Cat Girl } members of The Heroes
Superflash Gordon
Two photographers
Four TV announcers
Guinevere
Lancelot
Arthur
1st Children's Show presenter
2nd Children's Show presenter
3rd Children's Show presenter (Jeremy)
1st hoodlum
2nd hoodlum
Girl in trouble
Detective Itchy
Sergeant Crutch
Nick Bethjain (alias Jack)
Mrs Jones
Mr Jones
Boy
1st girl } their children
2nd girl
Girlfriend
Catering Manageress

Employment Officer
Landlady
Council Official
Mother
1st Police Officer
2nd Police Officer

The action takes place in a downtown neighbourhood

Time—the present

INTRODUCTION

You, Me and Mrs Jones was originally written to be performed by the Bournemouth Youth Theatre Enthusiasts—BYTE—at the Studio Theatre, Bournemouth Centre for Community Arts, in February 1986. The BYTE is different from many youth theatre groups in that almost all its public performances arise from the ideas of the members themselves—games and discussions lead to improvisations and more discussions. Eventually a dramatic framework is devised to link all the contributions together to make one play. With a clear plot outlined—and accepted by the members of the group—the script can be written.

You, Me and Mrs Jones was conceived in this manner. After seven weeks of workshop sessions with the BYTE I went away and wrote the play. As soon as it was finished parts were distributed and rehearsals began, more or less as they would with any production—only in this case a good deal of work had already been done on characterization. If *You, Me and Mrs Jones* is a play that has something positive—and humorous—to say about life for young people today this is due in large measure to the energy and enthusiasm of the BYTE members, aged between fourteen and seventeen years.

The story-line, which follows two ordinary teenagers on a quest for heroes "fit to save the day" through the murky worlds of street gangs, cranky religious sects, pop stars, television characters and vagrants should have plenty to offer youth theatres and school groups looking for a challenge.

You, Me and Mrs Jones is ideally suited for production "in the round", with the audience on four sides, separated by four corner entrances/exits. The original production used only one composite set—mainly consisting of one- and two-foot rostra blocks placed centrally to form a raised area. Obviously the play could be performed using more conventional theatre forms. But it would be a shame to lose the unique intimacy and immediacy between actors and audience afforded by an arena production. In my experience young people often take more naturally to this style of playing than working on a proscenium stage.

The large number of characters in the play should not be too off-putting. The idea behind this was to give as many actors as possible an opportunity to take part—and not just as extras. In fact the play has been written in such a way as to allow extensive doubling (and even trebling) if desired. The original BYTE cast was nineteen—ten male and nine female. This balance can easily be adjusted to suit the needs of a particular group—most of the characters can be played by members of either sex without the need for girls to pretend to be boys and vice versa.

Music for the Songs. In our original production the music used was not original, although of course it could have been. If you use tunes that are copyright (and please check this very carefully) do read the notice from the Performing Right Society on page iv. However, I like the idea that any groups performing the play should work out their own music!

What Does It Take To Be Truly Brave? was recited to an accompaniment of a Bach organ cantata, although again, of course, please feel free to be original.

One final note—although *You, Me and Mrs Jones* is a comedy, it is making a serious statement as well. It is important that the actors play the text straight and do not "send it up" in search of quick, easy laughs. The play will only work if the central characters believe in their "mission".

Tony Horitz

Director of BYTE and member of the Drama-in-Education Team at Bournemouth Centre for Community Arts

A licence issued by Samuel French Ltd to perform this play does not include permission to use any Incidental music specified in this copy. Where the place of performance is already licensed by the PERFORMING RIGHT SOCIETY a return of the music used must be made to them. If the place of performance is not so licensed then application should be made to the Performing Right Society, 29 Berners Street, London W1.

A separate and additional licence from PHONOGRAPHIC PERFORMANCES LTD, 1 Upper James Street, London W1R 3HG is needed whenever commercial recordings are used.

YOU, ME AND MRS JONES*

Scene 1

A Meeting With Jack

A dustbin, covered and overflowing with rubbish is placed c *and spotlit*

As the Scene opens strange, eerie music starts quietly and grows louder

From different corners two masked characters—Nobody and No one enter. Nobody—male—is searching for food. No one—female—is looking for somewhere to sleep. Eventually they approach the dustbin from different sides. Just as they get close to it the music stops and the Lights change

A strange character—Jack—leaps up from inside the dustbin, wearing the "rubbish" like a vast poncho

Jack Welcome!

Nobody and No one scream

I have been expecting you.

Pause

No one Me?
Nobody Me?
Jack Both of you.
Nobody I don't know her.
No one I don't know him.
Jack It doesn't matter. You both approached the bin.
Nobody I was hungry.
No one I was tired.
Jack I was waiting. For you. The chosen ones!

Pause

No one What?
Nobody You must be mistaken, mate. Confusing me with another bloke. I'm not from these parts, see. I've come down here to look for a job.
No one And I just wanted to get away from home.
Jack I have work for both of you.
Nobody Yeah? You're really offering us a job?

Jack Of the highest importance.
Nobody That's great! (*He cheers then changes mood*). Hey, you're not joking, are you?
Jack Do I look like I'm joking?
Nobody It's just that I've been on the dole for ages, see, and so . . .
Jack You talk too much. The mission I am sending you on involves the eyes, not the vocal chords.
Nobody (*eagerly*) Well what is it, then? I can't wait to start!
Jack You must go forth. Into this ancient land, troubled with sickness and sorrow, sullied with poverty and despair, wracked with anger, violence and decay. You must go forth. To search for heroes!
No one Heroes?
Jack I need heroes—to save the country!
Nobody I'm a bit confused. What sort of heroes do you mean?
Jack True ones—in the classical mould. Like the brave warriors of old who set out to perform impossible tasks, who fought all manner of evil, fearless and passionate.
Nobody Oh. One of those. (*Pause*) I'm not sure I'm cut out for this job—I've only got two "O" Levels.
Jack Enough! It's time for you to leave.
Nobody (*indicating No one*) Is she coming too?
Jack Of course. You and she are as one.
Nobody I can't see her being much use. Not at this job. She looks like she wouldn't say boo to a granny.
Jack Silence! Go and find the heroes. Bring them to me. Only you stand between salvation and the abyss.
Nobody But I'm Nobody.
No one And I'm No one.
Jack Exactly! You have been Nobody and No one. But now you shall be Somebody and Some one. You are together. Inextricably linked until you complete this quest.
Nobody (*Somebody*) Pardon?
No one (*Some one*) He means you can't get away from me.
Somebody I know—so you can talk after all!
Jack You have your instructions. You must carry them out. (*He begins to sink back into his bin*)
Some one Wait! I'm a coward . . . I'm afraid . . . of spiders . . . of opening my mouth in case a stupid word pops out . . . of a tap on my shoulder . . . I'm afraid . . .
Jack You have been chosen.
Some one . . . of you! I'm afraid of you!
Somebody Who are you?
Jack I am Jack.
Some one Jack who?
Jack Jack-in-the-bin.
Somebody Silly of us to ask really.
Some one How will we find you again?

Scene 2

Jack I will be here. In this street. Tonight — at sunset. Your mission must be accomplished by then (*He disappears back inside the bin*)
Somebody He's gone.
Some one Disappeared.

Pause

Somebody Well then . . . we'd better start, hadn't we?
Some one Yes. I suppose so.
Somebody Which way shall we go first?
Some one Just a . . .
Somebody (*interrupting*) I know! (*He points off*) Let's go that way! (*He moves*) Come on!
Some one Shouldn't we make a proper plan first? Draw up a list of possibilities?
Somebody No, no, no. We've got to be decisive . . . just follow me . . . I'll see you're all right. Hurry up!

He exits

Some one Just my luck to get saddled with an MCP Grade One!

She exits after him

Black-out

Scene 2

At Legless Lenny's

Three members of a gang — The 'Ell Raisers — enter, each shouting out his or her name as they circle the acting area menacingly

Zap Zap!
Pow Pow!
Crunch Crunch!
Zap Zap!
Pow Pow!
Crunch Crunch!
Zap Zap!
Pow Pow!
Crunch Crunch!

They freeze as they hear Some one and Somebody approaching. At a signal from Zap they "hide" in separate corners

Some one and Somebody enter

Somebody Come on! Stop dragging your feet.
Some one I don't like it here. It's too dark. Even our shadows look like ghosts.

Zap, Pow and Crunch sneak up and surround them

Somebody Don't talk daft! I rather like it. It reminds me of my home district. Stop worrying! Nothing's going to happen.
Zap Gotcha!
Some one Help!
Pow Who are you?
Somebody Er . . . I'm Somebody.
Crunch Don't get smart with us, Zit-face!
Pow 'Else we'll make you sing something simple! (*He hits him*)
Somebody Ouch!
Some one Stop it!
Zap Shut your clap-trap! What are you doing here? This is our territory.
Pow
Crunch } (*together*) Yeah! You're on our pitch, Snitch!
Zap Spill the beans, wind-bags! What are you after?
Some one We're looking for heroes.
Pow
Crunch } (*together*) For what?
Zap Heroes?
Somebody That's right, mateys.
Pow Here, Zap — do you hear? He's from up North!
Crunch Yuk!
Zap One of the unemployed millions probably.
Pow Come down here to pinch our jobs.
Crunch Yuk!
Somebody You don't understand!
Zap Oh yes we do! You cheeky clog-dancer!
Pow Let's chop his nose off!
Crunch Nail his ears to a tree!
Pow Aren't any trees growing round this area, Crunch.
Crunch Oh. I forgot that. (*Pause*) Let's stick 'em on a lamp post instead. (*He laughs*)
Somebody Steady on, lads!
Zap Do you know who you're dealing with, slime slug?
Somebody Er . . . no.
Zap Tell 'em, gang.
Pow
Crunch } (*together strongly*) Legless Lenny's 'Ell Raisers. That's who!
Zap We're tough on the streets!
Pow We're mean!
Crunch We're nasty!
Zap
Pow } (*together*) Understand?
Crunch
Some one We understand.
Somebody I bet you're not that tough!
Zap
Pow } (*together, closing in*) We're the 'Ell Raisers! (*They take out razors*
Crunch   *and brandish them menacingly*) Geddit?

Scene 2

Some one (*pulling Somebody away*) Listen, we don't mean any harm. It's been really nice talking to you, but we have to be going now. I don't think you're the heroes we're looking for, so . . .
Zap Stop them!
Pow (*blocking their exit*) You're not going anywhere!
Crunch Except underground! (*They laugh*) Can we do them over now, Zap?

They raise their arms and boots ready to attack Somebody and Some one

> *At that moment Legless Lenny arrives, being pushed on a small trolley on wheels by his girl, Lethal Lena*

Lenny Hold it, 'Ell Raisers! Zap! Pow! Crunch! I said stop!
Zap It's Lenny!
Pow }
Crunch } (*together*) Our beloved leader. (*They run over to him and fawn over him*)
Zap (*to Somebody and Some one*) And that's his devoted companion: Lethal Lena!
Somebody Who?
Pow }
Crunch } (*together*) Lethal Lena! If you don't watch it, she'll lean on you! (*They laugh raucously*)

Lenny Pow! Crunch!
Pow }
Crunch } (*together*) Yes, Lenny?
Lenny Cut the wise cracks! Who are these two?
Zap Just some nobody.
Pow }
Crunch } (*together*) And a little no one!
Somebody I'm Somebody now. And she's Some one!
Lenny Did I hear you say you were looking for a hero?
Some one Yes.
Lenny Well, you've come to the right place. Haven't they, Lena?
Lena Yes, Lenny.
Lenny I'm your hero, aren't I, 'Ell Raisers?
All Yes, Lenny.
Lena You're the best, Lenny.
Lenny I'm the toughest of the lot. (*He snaps his fingers*) Fierce as a ferret.
Zap Brave as a badger.
Pow Harder than a hippo.
Crunch Touchier than a tarantula.
Lena Yeah!
Lenny What you staring at? My legs?
Some one No! We didn't even notice you hadn't got any!
Zap Don't be so rude!
Pow }
Crunch } (*together*) You naughty little noggin.
Lenny We'll show them, 'Ell Raisers. Show them how I lost my legs.

All 'Ell Raisers We'll show them.
Lenny Then you'll understand why I'm a hero.
All Then they'll know.
Lenny I'm going to tell you a little story. And the gang will do a spot of criminal reconstruction. (*He orders Zap, Pow and Crunch*) Move them out of the way!

The gang move Somebody and Some one to the side

Lena! You may portray me in this story. Doing just what I did. To your positions, 'Ell Raisers!

They spread out and take up statuesque poises, ready to mime the story that Lenny tells. They play objects — like pub doors and shop windows — and people, as described. Even Lenny's metaphors — such as the image of squirming ants lying on their backs — should be portrayed simply and unemotionally by the 'Ell Raisers

Lenny Once upon a time. Late on a Saturday night. After midnight. The pubs are shut. I'm walking alone along the back streets of town. Look in the shop windows. Boring. I feel very bored. Suddenly! I see an old fogey doddering along in front of me. So I think I'll do him over. See how much money he's got on him. Easy! I sneak up behind him. Doesn't spot a thing. A quick left to his kidneys; a right in his gut and down he goes! Like a burst paper bag. I grab his wallet and I'm off. But wait! Who's that lot coming towards me over the road as I make my weary way to the square? Oh no! It can't be ... can it? Yes, it is! Oh no! It's the HGVs!
Zap
Pow } (*together*) The Highly Gifted in Violence Gang!
Crunch
Lenny The HGVs! Deadly rivals to the 'Ell Raisers from the neighbouring town. And it's me they're after. They get closer. There must be hundreds of them. Their eyes are blazing hot with hideous hate. Their muscles are bulging like bloated bullocks. They come really close. But I don't flinch! I'm ready. With a catherine wheel whirl my legs spiral through space, lighting up the night. I take out one ... two ... three ... four! They tumble like skittles into the dark alleys of the town. But still they come at me. With cutters, hammers, axes, milk bottles. I fell them all. Leave them in a heap. Squirming ants what have been scalded by my boiling waters. And I'm away again — laughing — into the early morning.
Somebody (*jumping up, enthusiastically*) That was great, mate! What a story! There is one thing, though. If you beat them all ... how come you lost your legs?
Lenny I got hit by a lorry, didn't I? As I was walking away from the fight.

The gang form up into a lorry and knock Lena — as Lenny — over

Zap
Pow } (*together*) An HGV!
Crunch
Lenny All right, you cruds! You don't need to remind me.

Scene 2

Zap
Pow } (*together*) Sorry, Lenny.
Crunch
Lena Here, you two. (*To Some one and Somebody*) Is my Lenny the hero you're looking for?
Somebody I reckon he is.
Some one We'll just have to have a little discussion.

They whisper together

The 'Ell Raisers go and fawn around Lenny again

Excuse me ... we so enjoyed that last part of the story ... we'd like to watch it again.
Lenny Like it, eh?
Some one } (*together*) Yes!
Somebody
Lenny They liked it, 'Ell Raisers.
Zap
Pow } (*together*) Shall we show them again, Lenny?
Crunch
Lenny Yeah. Then we'll do them over. All right, 'Ell Raisers?
Zap
Pow } (*together*) Yeah. Then we'll do them.
Crunch
Lenny (*beginning the story again*) It's Saturday night. After twelve. The pubs shut. I'm walking. Along the street.

While they act Some one sneaks off pulling Somebody after her

I pass a shop window, boring. Bored. See an old fogey ahead. I sneak up. Think. I'll do him over. Easy. One, two, three. (*He turns to Some one and Somebody*) Hey, are you two watching this? Eh! Where have they gone?
Zap They've hopped it!
Pow } (*together*) Legged it, Lenny!
Crunch
Lenny After them, 'Ell Raisers.

They rush off

Wait for me!
Lena Lena's here, Lenny. Lean on me. I love you, Lenny.
Lenny I want those two alive!

They exit

Music

Black-out

SCENE 3

In Another Street

Some one enters, running. Somebody follows

Some one Come on! Quick!
Somebody Stop! Hang on a minute, will you?
Some one No time. They're after us.
Somebody Nonsense.
Some one They'll kill us.
Somebody You're being hysterical.
Some one I'm not! You ...
Somebody (*interrupting*) Listen to me for a change!
Some one Huh! (*She stops moving and faces him*)
Somebody What did you want to up and run off like that for?
Some one Because they were going to hurt us.
Somebody No they weren't. They were just being friendly.
Some one Call that friendly?
Somebody Of course! Having a little joke with us.
Some one They were high on violence. Aggro-addicts.
Somebody A bit of a laugh, that's all. And you went and ruined everything.
Some one I saved us.
Somebody You chickened out—and lost us our heroes.
Some one No.
Somebody Yes! (*He turns away*) Legless Lenny! What a guy! The way he took on the HGV mob single-handed. Amazing! (*To Some one*) He scared you, didn't he?
Some one He was just a moron. A big mouth in charge of a load of rotten teeth. That's all. A head case with no luggage in it.
Somebody Well I reckon he was the hero Jack's after.
Some one So go back, then. Go on. If you're so sure.
Somebody Where?
Some one Back to Lenny's.
Somebody All right. I think I will. Come on.
Some one Oh, no. I'm not risking it.
Somebody But remember what Jack said—we've got to stick together.
Some one He'll understand. You seem to act as if you don't need me anyway. So now's your chance to prove it.
Somebody You reckon you know it all, don't you? So clever.
Some one No, I don't but ...
Somebody Yeah, well, I am going back for Lenny. Rather him than you any day. Jack made a big mistake assigning you to this mission. All you do is criticize. Why can't you trust people? Like me. You're superior, you are, you don't believe in anything, you've got no faith, you ...

He runs off. Pause

Some one Oh dear. Perhaps he's right. I do always see the dark side. But

Scene 3

that's my nature. I wish I could trust people like he does. Have faith in something, but . . .

Unseen, a strange character, McConnemmall, enters. He—or she—stands watching Some one

McConnemmall T-t-t-t-t! Oh dear, oh dear, oh dear, my dear!
Some one (*frightened*) Huh!
McConnemmall Do not be alarmed. I will not hurt you.
Some one Who are you?
McConnemmall McConnemmall's the name. I could not help hearing what you were saying. You poor, poor girl. I do understand. I felt just like you once.
Some one Really?
McConnemmall Yes, really and truly. I know you will find it hard to believe.
Some one I do.
McConnemmall You see! (*Declaiming*) Oh ye of little faith! Lost soul! You are tired of the material world, child, are you not?
Some one Yes, yes I am.
McConnemmall What a cruel place it can be, indeed! A swamp of silent, solitary suffering. A billowing sheet torn to shreds by the sharp steel of violence and desperation. Where is love, I ask? Where is love?
Some one Yes. That's what I wonder as well.
McConnemmall (*moving very close to her*) My poor, poor child. You need faith, you seek hope. Am I right?
Some one Yes. I reckon I'll have to give up this search.
McConnemmall (*with interest*) And what search would that be, my dear?
Some one For heroes. I'm supposed to be looking for heroes.
McConnemmall And you want to give up your quest? Not so fast, not so fast, sweet child. There is hope at the end of the long night of the soul.
Some one How strangely you talk.
McConnemmall I have come here to lead you towards the new morning.
Some one I'd like to trust you, but . . .
McConnemmall I understand your doubt. Do not be afraid. Come with me now. I will lead you to the one you have been seeking.
Some one A hero?
McConnemmall Oh yes, my pilgrim. A hero of the spirit. It is time to say goodbye to dull, useless material values—did you say you had a large amount of money?
Some one Just my savings. And what my mother gave me to last until I got a job.
McConnemmall You will not need any of that trash any more. We will unburden you of its heavy leaden weight. (*He stands and takes her hand*) Follow, child, follow.
Some one Where are we going?
McConnemmall To our tent. Follow!

He leads her off

Pause. We hear chanting

Somebody enters from the other side, looking rather crestfallen

Somebody Some one, I've been thinking. I suppose I shouldn't have run off like that. I ought to have listened to you. I changed my mind. About Lenny. Maybe you were right. Yeah, maybe he was a bit of a ... Some one? I've come back. To protect you. Some one? She's gone. What a nerve! (*He looks around and hears chanting offstage*) Funny noise. Seems to be coming from that tent. I'd better have a look.

He exits in the same direction as Some one and McConnemmall

Black-out

Scene 4

Inside The Booties tent

A procession of Booties enter, ready to begin their ceremony. They are dressed in identical robes and wear a silvery pendant shaped like a boot around their neck. The Leader is carrying a large silver boot, mounted on a cushion

Leader Holey Bootie, Holey Bootie, how we love thee, Holey Bootie!
Booties Holey Bootie, Holey Bootie, how we love thee, Holey Bootie!

Leader places the silver Boot reverentially on a central block

The Booties make a circle around it

Leader Oh Holey Boot, we worship thee.
Booties Oh Holey Boot, we worship thee.
Leader Up on our toes and on bended knee.
Booties Up on our toes and on bended knee.

McConnemmall enters with Some one. They stand and watch

Leader In the Holey Boot we find the sole. We prostrate ourselves before the beautiful Boot.

The Booties all lie down on their stomachs with arms outstretched towards the Boot

Booties Oh beautiful Boot.

They lift up the bottom half of their legs and hold them still as Leader moves around inspecting them

Leader Feel it, Booties. Feel the firm yet feather-light imprint of the Boot upon it. Without it we are as nothing—naked—our blisters, our corns, our verrucae the outward signs of our misery, our sole's torment.

The Booties roll over onto their backs and raise their legs

Booties We feel the imprint of the Boot upon us.

Scene 4

Leader Let it trample on your past lives, erase your material wickedness. Let the weight of the Boot crush all doubt.

The Booties begin bicycling with their legs

Booties Let the Boot crush all doubt! Let the Boot crush all doubt!

McConnemmall steps forward and stops the proceedings

McConnemmall Brothers and sisters of the Boot—your attention!

The Booties stand up

We have a new recruit to our ranks. Praise be to the Boot!
Booties (*stamping their feet*) Praise be to the Boot!
Leader Welcome, stranger. What is your name?
Some one Some one.
Leader Do you really wish to join our ranks?
Some one I'm not sure. I think so.
Leader You will be sure soon. We shall crush all doubt, shan't we, Booties?
Booties We shall crush all doubt! (*They stamp their feet again*)
Leader (*drawing Some one in towards the Boot*) Look at the Boot, Some one. See how it shines. (*He carefully picks up the Boot*) See the hope it offers to those who embrace its leathery love.
Some one (*half-convinced*) I'm looking!
Leader Have you been living in the vale of sorrow for long, child?
McConnemmall (*answering for her*) She has, she has!
Some one Well... yes.
Leader Aren't you tired of all this aggravation? Of the lies?
Some one I am tired.
Leader She is ready for the Boot!
Booties Give her the Boot!

At a sign from the Leader they all start swaying gently from side to side. As the scene builds, the swaying grows faster and faster

The Leader hands the Boot carefully to the first Bootie who lifts it to his nose, sniffs, breathes deeply and then passes the Boot on to the next in line. The process is repeated during the next speeches until the Boot has completed the circle and is held by McConnemmall, poised above Some one's head

Leader You are a little girl lost in the dark.
McConnemmall With no one to turn to.
Some one No one.
Leader The child has no one to speak to.
Some one It's true!
Leader She needs help, consolation.
McConnemmall She needs the Boot!
Booties She needs the Boot!
Leader She is weighed down with filthy lucre.
McConnemmall Your money, your money!
Leader If only she could be free.

Booties She needs the Boot!
Some one I need the Boot.
Leader Stop!

Everyone freezes as McConnemmall now holds the Boot above Some one's outstretched arm

Renounce your tragic past!
McConnemmall Give us your money!

Dazed, Some one produces a purse which she hands to McConnemmall

Somebody enters and stands watching

Leader See Booties! She has renounced all her worldly sins!
Booties Praise be to the Boot!

They all kneel and start tapping on the ground

Somebody What's all this mumbo-jumbo?

Leader hands Some one the Boot. She gazes at it with love, holding it above her head like a trophy

Leader Feel it moving, tighter and tighter. The Power of the Boot!
Booties The Power of the Boot!
Leader Do you feel it?
Some one I feel it! I feel it!
Leader You are free!
Some one I feel free! I feel free!
McConnemmall You have found what you were looking for.
Some one I have found my hero—the hero for Jack!

Somebody rushes forward and intervenes

Somebody Stop!

The Booties' tapping now becomes drumming as they build up to a climax

I said stop! STOP!

The Booties stop. There is silence

Leave her alone! She's with me! You've ripped her off—I saw you take her money (*He grabs Some one, who resists*) Come on!
Some one No! I have found freedom!
Somebody You're dreaming. They've conned you.
Some one (*declaiming*) Long live the Boot!
Somebody I'm taking you with me!
Some one (*struggling*) Let go of me! I hate you!

Somebody drags her offstage

Leader (*to McConnemmall*) Who was that geezer?
McConnemmall I don't know.
Leader You don't suppose he was the Law?

Scene 4

McConnemmall We'd better make ourselves scarce just in case.
Leader (*to The Booties*) Follow me, Booties. By the left ... hop! Holey Bootie, Holey Bootie, how we love you, Holey Bootie!

The Booties follow McConnemmall and the Leader offstage, chanting

Black-out

Scene 5

In The Street

Somebody enters pulling Some one behind him

Somebody We've got to carry on with the search ... to find the heroes!
Some one I have found—the Boot!
Somebody Stuff the Boot! That's just hocus-pocus.
Some one You have destroyed my happiness.
Somebody (*aside*) I don't believe this! Not long ago you were throwing cold water words on my passions! We seem to be changing around. What's happening?
Some one I am free! Nothing scares me any more! (*Loudly*) I have found my voice!
Somebody Oh blimey! She's in a trance. How can I get her out of it?

Three fans rush across the stage and knock into Somebody

Steady on!
1st Fan Sorry, mate. We're in a bit of a hurry.
Somebody So I noticed. You aren't anything to do with Legless Lenny's mob, are you?
2nd Fan Who?
Somebody Never mind. Where are you going?
3rd Fan The gig, of course.
Somebody What gig?
2nd Fan At the Hippodrome.
Somebody Who's playing?
Fans "The Heroes".
Somebody What! Are they a band?
3rd Fan Don't you know anything? They're amazing!
1st Fan } (*together*) They're fantastic!
2nd Fan }
3rd Fan The best sound in town.
1st Fan And they're doing a gig in aid of the unemployed.
2nd Fan Yeah, 'cos they're very concerned, see.
Somebody They really are heroes, then?
Fans Don't miss them! Bye!

They run off

Somebody (*to Some one*) We've struck lucky at last! It must be right,

Some one A concert for the unemployed . . . "The Heroes". Must be the ones Jack's after.
Some one Nothing is real, only the Boot.
Somebody Oh no! Well, you are coming with me to this gig, whether you like it or not. Let's have you on your feet.

He pulls her up and off, after the Fans

Black-out

Scene 6

Outside The Hippodrome

Bouncer enters with a large bill board advertising the concert by "The Heroes", which he sets down in front of the "entrance"

Bouncer Come along now, kids. This way in to "The Heroes" concert. See them live. Come on, get your tickets ready. Let's not have any hassle. On stage shortly, the fabulous, phenomenological "Heroes", idols and superstars!

Three Fans hurry on and approach Bouncer with tickets

Easy does it, darling. Don't overexcite yourself. Let's see your ticket.
1st Fan I can't wait. (*She gives her ticket in*)
Bouncer I bet you can't, love. (*To the next in the queue*) And the next.
2nd Fan (*handing in her ticket*) Where do we buy the programmes?
Bouncer Right inside, darling. Programmes, pickies, posters, pendants, peanuts, plastic bath toys—we've got the lot! Make sure you spend all your money—it's all in a good cause. Next, please!
3rd Fan I hope I manage to touch Gordon.
Bouncer Careful, love, you might catch something! Only joking, gorgeous. And the next!

Somebody enters with Some one behind, still holding the Boot

Some one Holey Bootie, Holey Bootie, how we love thee, Holey Bootie.
Bouncer Hallo, hallo, hallo! What have we got here? Booze or Uhu?
Somebody Don't take any notice of her. We want to see "The Heroes" play.
Bouncer Well I want to see your tickets then, my old fruit (*he glances at Some one*) and nut.
Somebody We haven't got any.
Bouncer Haven't got any? Tut-tut! Ticket Office is right over there.
Somebody Ah yes . . . but we haven't any money left to pay for them.
Bouncer Oh deary me! Well, you won't be able to see the band then.
Somebody But . . .
Bouncer Sorry, Hard-luck Henry. You aren't allowed in without a ticket.
Somebody But isn't this gig supposed to be in aid of the unemployed?
Bouncer Correct, Clever Clogs. So?
Somebody Well, we're both unemployed, so we ought to get in free.
Bouncer Now you're being a silly billy. If we were to let in all the

Scene 7

unemployed free, how would we ever raise any money for the unemployed kids who can't afford to get in to concerts?
Somebody That doesn't make sense.
Bouncer (*angrily*) Are you incinerating that I'm a bit on the thick side, sonny?
Somebody No, it's just that ... look, I suppose I'd better tell you the truth so you'll understand. The fact is, we've been sent on this really very important mission ...
Bouncer You don't say?
Somebody Yes. And we've got to find a hero by sunset or ...
Bouncer Or disaster will strike?
Somebody Well, yes.
Bouncer Leave it out, mush! That's what they all say—any old excuse'll do for that bouncer! But they're wrong. You're wrong. I'm no dip-stick, so save your tricks! You are not coming in without a ticket and that is final.
Somebody You must let us in!
Some one He needs the Boot!
Bouncer I'll give you the boot if you don't clear off! Now hop it!

Bouncer picks up the bill-board and exits

Somebody There must be a way to get in. Let's try round the back.
Some one The Boot knows every way.
Somebody Put a sock in it! Come on, let's hurry!

They exit

Black-out

SCENE 7

Inside The Hippodrome

In the Black-out all the Fans—the whole company of actors—rush in noisily to the front of "the stage" and start cheering and gesticulating excitedly

The Announcer runs on and leaps onto a raised rostrum above them. At a signal from him the Fans freeze

Announcer Hi there, hero worshippers! How are you doing? You are in for a real treat today, OK? And we all know why, or do I lie? Who's the best band in town with the bestest sound?
Fans (*coming to life*) "The Heroes"!
Announcer The who?
Fans No, "The Heroes"!
Announcer I can hear you, teeny-droppers, but the band can't! You want them to come out and play, don't you, droolers?
Fans "The Heroes"! We want "The Heroes"!
Announcer That's better! OK, OK, OK. Let's hear your hysteria for all the band: first, to thrill you with the daring clashing of his colourful costume, The Electric Crusader!

The Electric Crusader runs on and takes up a dramatic pose

Next, shiver your livers, 'cos it's Thunder Woman!

Thunder Woman, appropriately dressed, runs on and takes up a pose

To complete the backing group, the purr-fect purr-former in purr-son. It's Cat Girl!

Cat Girl runs on and takes up a pose

And finally, fans, the biggest superstar of them all, yes, it's me! (*He pulls off his long coat to reveal a "Superhero" costume underneath*). Superflash Gordon! Let's hear the music, man!

The music for Song 1 begins

Gordon sings solo and the others sing chorus

Song 1

Gordon   Something is happening in the streets today
Tension's growing stronger
It just won't go away!
Fear and hatred, violent despair
Have crept up from the gutters
You can smell them everywhere!

Chorus

Group   We need heroes
Listen to what we say!
We need heroes
To come and save the day!

Repeat

Gordon   Now there's fighting and burning in the streets today
The people growing angry
They just won't go away.
Tired of religion, fed up with TV
We gotta give them something so
Why don't they turn to me?

Chorus

Group   We're your heroes
Listen to what we say!
We're your heroes
We've come to save the day!

Repeat

The Fans cheer ecstatically then freeze

Somebody appears from nowhere and goes right up onto the rostrum next to Gordon

Scene 7

Somebody At last! "The Heroes!" You have to be the ones! Yes! Quick, all of you, pack up your things and follow me to Jack.
Gordon (*to the group*) Who is this berk?
Somebody I'm Somebody, I've come to ...
Gordon I don't care if you're Cliff Richard, you can't interrupt our gigs!

Some one suddenly appears

Some one Only The Boot! Only The Boot is the real hero!
Bouncer (*running after her*) Come back here!
Gordon Get rid of these intruders!
Bouncer Come on, you sneaky scum-bags. Out!

All the Fans boo and hiss Somebody and Some one as they are escorted out

Gordon It's all over, fans, don't worry!

The Fans are silent

Some people just don't know how to behave in public. Never mind, we won't let them spoil our fun. Our next number is especially dedicated to all the unemployed of the land. I mean, like ... it's really heavy, isn't it? I know. We all know. We've been there. We know what it's like ... and we don't like what we know. But all you poor unemployed people out there, if you managed to scrape up the price of a ticket, remember. Remember, we care. Buy our next album and ... well, it may help. Us. And you. Here's the song. One, two, three, four ...

The music for Song 2 begins. Again, Gordon sings vocals and the group sing chorus The Fans turn outwards and assume aggressive, fighting postures. During the song they mime martial arts actions. They join in the final chorus

Song 2: Song of the Unemployed

(*Singing*) It's a real drag being unemployed
Makes you feel down and extremely annoyed
We've all suffered and we know what it's like
When they say "Get off your bum and on your bike!"

We're the heroes of the unemployed
The only ones who really care,
We'll keep on singing our wonderful songs
Just for you, the jobless ones ...

Chorus

Group Heroes ... of the unemployed
Heroes ... of the unemployed

Group and fans Heroes ... unemployed!
Heroes ... unemployed!
Heroes ... unemployed!
Heroes!

Black-out
Music

Scene 8

Back in the street outside

Somebody and Some one are thrown onstage by Bouncer

Bouncer (*off*) And don't try sneaking back in! Stay in the gutter where you belong!
Somebody You don't understand! I must speak to the band!
Some one Life is like a boot. Shining and hard on the outside. But inside— hollow. (*She sits*)
Somebody Yeah. And sometimes it smells rotten. (*He sits*) How am I ever going to finish this job by sunset now? And how am I going to unbrainwash your booted-up head.

Pause

From another side of the acting area "The Heroes" sneak out by the "back door" of the Hippodrome

Gordon Quick, Heroes—out through the back door; no revolting fans in sight. Better make a break for it.

Two Photographers come on from the other side, just as the rest of "The Heroes" come on stage behind Gordon

Oh no! Photographers! What it is to be famous, eh?
1st Photographer Just a few snaps, folks!
2nd Photographer Got to give the punters what they want!

"The Heroes" automatically form themselves into a "star-type" pose and freeze as the Photographers take pictures

Thunder Woman Hey, Gordon, how much money did we make then?
Cat Girl Yeah, I was wondering about that, too.
Gordon Quite a bit. Ten or eleven thousand, I reckon.
Crusader What about all this unemployed stuff?
Gordon What about it?

They change to a different pose

1st Photographer Nearly finished, "Heroes".
2nd Photographer Keep smiling!
Crusader Aren't we supposed to be giving the money to them?
Gordon Who?
Crusader To them. The unemployed.
Gordon Well, yeah, we are. Sort of. But only a donation. To help pay for a social centre they want to open round here.
Cat Girl So how much do we give them? A thousand?
Photographers Thanks "Heroes"!

The Photographers leave

Gordon A thousand? Don't be silly. We ain't the Samaritans. Five hundred'll do.

Scene 8

Somebody moves over to them and intervenes

Somebody Excuse me, "Heroes", but that isn't fair. You must give them all of it.
Thunder Woman What's it to you, busy-body?
Somebody You advertised it, talked about it at the concert. Everyone thinks you're giving all the money to the unemployed.
Gordon But we are, mate. Five hundred pounds. And very generous too.
Somebody What about the other nine thousand five hundred?
Gordon What about it?
Crusader That's for our expenses.
Cat Girl Yeah! We've got very big expenses.
Somebody I don't believe it. You must give it all away. Then I can take you to meet Jack.
Cat Woman Look at the time! We really must be going.
Gordon Yes. (*He points*) There's our chauffeur waiting for us!
Somebody (*blocking their way*) No! I won't let you go!
Gordon Bouncer! Where are you?

Bouncer appears at another corner

Bouncer Here I am. What's bugging you, folks?
Heroes (*pointing to Somebody*) He is!
Gordon Deal with him, would you?
Cat Woman There's a good chap.
Heroes (*to Somebody as they leave*) See you!

They exit

Bouncer steps forward, looking threatening

Bouncer So it's you again? I told you to stay away. Didn't I?
Somebody Yes, but ...
Bouncer I'll give you butts ... (*He head butts him*) And this is for being a naughty little boy ... (*He hits him in the stomach*) ... and not taking uncle Bouncer's advice ... (*He kicks him up his posterior*)

Somebody falls onto the rostrum block

(*Lifting up his head*) There! Next time, stay out of my way, eh? (*He bangs Somebody's head on the block*) He really thinks he's Somebody!

He leaves, wiping his hands

Pause

Somebody lies groaning

Suddenly, Some one drops the Boot and stands up. She walks over to Somebody and bends over him

Some one Are you ... ?
Somebody Alive? I don't know.

Pause

Some one I'm sorry.
Somebody What?
Some one Sorry. That they hurt you. I should have helped you.
Somebody No.
Some one I was too busy ... staring at the Boot.
Somebody Yes.
Some one I've changed, though. Suddenly, it all seems ... stupid.
Somebody (*rolling off the block*) I know what you mean.
Some one You were right about the Boot. It was a con.
Somebody Just like the band. Some heroes!
Some one Yes.
Somebody I've changed too. Life stinks. I know that much now. There are no real heroes. Only cheats and liars! (*Getting up*) Pass me that boot, will you?
Some one (*fetching the Boot*) Here you are. (*She gives it to him*)
Somebody This is what I think of the whole bunch of them! (*He moves to the side of the stage and throws the Boot off*)

We hear the sound of crashing glass

Some one (*after a pause*) You've broken a shop window.
Somebody I don't care.
Some one (*walking over to the "window"*) The shop's full of televisions. Some of them are switched on. Let's go in and watch one.
Somebody All right. I suppose it might take my mind off things a bit.

They start to leave

Hey, it could be dangerous to hang around here. Aren't you afraid of getting caught?
Some one What for?
Somebody I broke a shop window.
Some one It was an accident. Anyway, we've been told to find heroes so ...
Somebody Yes! I've got it! Heroes on the television! There must be thousands of them! Why didn't we think of that earlier?
Some one I did, actually.
Somebody (*interrupting*) Jack never said they had to be real, did he? Come on, Some one, no time to lose! This could be our last chance!

He exits

Some one Perhaps he hasn't changed that much after all.

She exits

Black-out

Scene 9

Inside The Television Shop

In the darkness, the noise of several television channels working at once can be made out faintly

Scene 9

Two Actors carrying a large blue blanket enter. They sit facing each other with the blanket stretched between them. It represents a river in the first programme

TV Announcer Just about to start on Channel A, "The Life and Loves of Queen Guinevere and Lancelot of the Lake", a classic tale of chivalry and romance.

Suitable music begins as

Guinevere enters alone

From another corner Some one and Somebody enter. They sit in a corner, in front of the "screen", which can be real or imaginary

Somebody Good, a programme's just starting.
Some one Look a gallant knight on horseback!

Lancelot gallops on and leaves his horse at the side of the acting area. He approaches Guinevere

Guinevere Ah, good Knight!
Lancelot But I've only just arrived!
Guinevere Darling Lancelot!
Lancelot Darling Guinevere! Your eyes sparkle like a bejewelled sword in the lake!
Guinevere Oh darling, yes! More!
Lancelot Your lips glisten like delicious cherries dangling from a magic tree!
Guinevere Oh yes! Pluck them at once! (*She pouts*)
Lancelot Darling Guinevere!
Guinevere Darling Lancelot!
Lancelot Oh, how I love you, Guinevere!
Guinevere Oh Lancelot, my heart is beating like a drum before battle.
Lancelot But I come to make love not war!
Guinevere Oh yes, my handsome knight! Madly and passionately!
Lancelot (*turning away dramatically*) But what about your husband, my Lord Arthur of Camelot?
Guinevere What of him? He has an icicle for a heart. And besides, he's always out at nights.
Lancelot (*taking her in his arms*) Oh, darling Guinevere!
Guinevere (*responding*) Oh darling Lancelot!

We hear the sound of thundering hooves as

Arthur enters on horseback. He parks his horse and draws his sword

Arthur So, you treacherous knight! I find you embracing my Guinevere!
Guinevere (*turning to the audience*) Oh no! Arthur home early! Zounds.
Arthur Draw your sword, Lancelot!
Lancelot (*doing so*) Certainly, my Lord!

As Lancelot finally raises his sword he knocks Guinevere off the block into the blanket — river — which nows begins to "rage". Unaware of Guinevere's plight, Arthur and Lancelot fight

Guinevere Oh! Help me! I am fallen into a raging river. Save me! I said help! I am sinking!

Lancelot and Arthur stop fighting

Lancelot Look! Guinevere! Poor dear, she is sinking in the raging river! I will save her!
Arthur No, you errant knight! I will save her!
Lancelot No, I will save her!
Arthur No, I will save her!
Lancelot Let us fight to decide who should save her!

They continue fighting, moving offstage

Guinevere in the blanket is carried offstage — upstream

Some one Typical men! Behaving like stupid kids.
Somebody No! It was a good fight, I reckon! (*Pause*) No, you're right. What a pair of wallies!
Some one Let's try another channel. (*She presses a button*)
Voice Over Next on Channel B our regular children's programme, "TV Time for Tiny-Winies".

Appropriate introductory music begins as

Two Presenters enter, bouncing

1st Presenter Bounce!
2nd Presenter Bounce!
1st Presenter Hallo, boys and girls!
2nd Presenter Hallo, everyone! Today on "TV Time for Tiny-Winies" we are going to pretend to be grown-ups.
1st Presenter And be ever so sensible.
2nd Presenter So are you watching very, very carefully?
Somebody ⎫
Some one ⎬ (*together*) Yes.
1st Presenter ⎫
2nd Presenter ⎬ (*together*) Good. Then let's pretend!

3rd Presenter enters, carrying a soft toy that looks like a lion

3rd Presenter Bounce!
1st Presenter Ooh, look! Here's Jeremy with Jemima!
2nd Presenter Hallo, Jemima! Hallo, Jeremy!
3rd Presenter Hallo, everybody! Can you guess what Jemima is today? I'll tell you — she's a dog!
1st Presenter Ooh! Woof, woof!
2nd Presenter Yes, boys and girls. Dogs go "Woof, woof", don't they?
3rd Presenter Yes, they do. They go "Woof, woof, woof".
1st Presenter I know a song about dogs.
2nd Presenter Do you?
1st Presenter Yes. Shall I sing it?
3rd Presenter What a super idea! Let's all sing it together!

Scene 9

1st Presenter All right then. After four . . .

Song 3

They sing to the tune and rhythm of "Frère Jacques" in a round

All We like dogs, we like dogs, we like dogs,
Doggies go woof, doggies go woof, woof,
We like dogs, we like dogs . . .

1st Presenter Wasn't that fun? (*He crinkles up his nose*) Oh dear! I think you'd better take Jemima for a walk outside the studio now, Jeremy. Bye-bye!
2nd Presenter Yes, bye-bye, Jeremy and Jemima!
3rd Presenter Bye for now!

He exits with Jemima

1st Presenter Well, what are we going to do next?
2nd Presenter Let's do some exercises!
1st Presenter Ooh, yes! Let's try and touch our toes five times!
2nd Presenter Yes! And all you boys and girls out there can touch your toes too! Up you get!

The music begins

Somebody and Some one stand and touch their toes at the same time as the two Presenters do

That was fun! Now, I know something else that is very very difficult for boys and girls to do.
1st Presenter And what's that?
2nd Presenter Behaving yourself when you go to the supermarket to do the shopping with mummy!
1st Presenter Gosh, yes! That is hard.
2nd Presenter But if you watch us carefully we'll show you how to do it properly.
1st Presenter I know a song about a supermarket.
2nd Presenter What a surprise!
1st Presenter Yes. Let's sing it together. I'll pretend to be mummy shopping. You can be a little boy or girl sitting in a trolley.
2nd Presenter But where's the trolley?

A trolley is sent on from offstage

1st Presenter There! On you get!

The 2nd Presenter sits on the trolley which the 1st Presenter wheels around as they sing. The 1st Presenter mimes shopping

Song 4

(*Singing*) When we go shopping we keep our hands to ourself

And we try not to be naughty
We leave all the cans quite alone on the shelf
And we don't keep on at our mummy.

We don't ask for ices or bickies or sweets
And we don't race around the store.
We just help our mum pack the veg and the meat
And behave like good little bores.

They go off waving to the audience

Some one I don't believe it! Not even little children can look up to those two.
Somebody They treated us like idiots! Some heroes they are!
Some one Try Channel C.
Voice Over And now crime raises its ugly head again in tonight's exciting episode of "The Boys in Blue on the Beat in the Streets of San Fernando."

The music begins

Somebody This is more like it! Crime fighting in the USA!

Two Hoodlums enter, looking shifty

Some one They look more like villains than goodies.
Somebody Ssssh! The cops'll be along soon.
1st Hoodlum I'm bored of just hanging around under this boardwalk.
2nd Hoodlum Yeah. This boardwalk's really boring.
1st Hoodlum So what we gonna do?
2nd Hoodlum Er . . . we're hoodlums, aren't we?
1st Hoodlum Yeah. We're the lowest of the low.
2nd Hoodlum So why don't we mug some poor, innocent passer-by?
1st Hoodlum Good idea. You got your mask?
2nd Hoodlum Yeah. (*He takes out his mask*) What you think?
1st Hoodlum That's really scarey. (*He takes out another mask*) What do you think of mine?
2nd Hoodlum That's really scarey.

We hear a noise off

Quick! A passer-by's just about to pass by. Let's hide in the shadows.

They hide

From the other side of the acting area a glamorous flouncy Girl enters

1st Hoodlum (*springing out to surprise her*) Hi there, floozy!
2nd Hoodlum (*springing out*) Hi there, doll.
Girl Oh! A pair of horrible low-life hoodlums! Help!
2nd Hoodlum Fancy a good time, darling?
1st Hoodlum Wanna boogie with us, baby?
Girl Get lost, you slimey bums! (*She hits the Hoodlums*)
2nd Hoodlum OK, lady, just for that we're gonna mug you!
1st Hoodlum Yeah! You asked for it, broad!

Scene 9

2nd Hoodlum Let's put on our masks so she won't recognize us later!
1st Hoodlum Good idea.

They put on their masks and start jostling the Girl

Girl Help! Why doesn't some macho cop or two come and rescue me!

The music begins

Two Cops, Itchy and Crutch, enter frenetically with their guns out. They rush to the "screen"

Itchy Hi there! We're the good guys! I'm Itchy!
Crutch I'm Crutch!
Itchy \
Crutch / (*together*) We're Supercops! The duo in blue!
Itchy When there's trouble in the streets!
Crutch We're on the scene.
Itchy We keep the precinct clean.
Crutch We're strong.
Itchy We're tough.
Crutch We help people.
Itchy People admire us.
Itchy \
Crutch / (*together*) We're cool. We're handsome. We're clean cut.

They freeze momentarily

Girl Help, help! You handsome, clean cut, cool, tough, strong cops!
Crutch Wow! That chick needs our help, Itchy.
Itchy Let's get in there, Crutch!

They rush up to the hoodlums

Hoodlums Oh no! It's Detective Itchy and Sergeant Crutch!

The music begins

They fight. Itchy and Crutch overcome the Hoodlums and chase them offstage

Some one More violence! They're as bad as Lenny and his 'Ell Raisers. (*Pause. To Somebody*) Or do you still reckon that's the sort of hero we need?
Somebody No. Goodies or baddies—what's the difference? Let's face it, Some one, we're wasting our time. We might as well pack it in.
Some one No. There's one more channel.
Somebody It'll be the same as ...
Some one Let's try it anyway. (*She changes channel*)
Voice Over And now on Channel D, "A Thought for Today" with Nick Bethjain.

We hear organ music

Somebody Funny name!

Some one Sssh!

A strange figure enters with a large book. He sits and looks at the audience

Nick Bethjain What does it take to be truly brave?

> To be truly brave
> Is not to raise
> The voice or fist
> In search of praise
>
> To be truly brave
> Is not to boast
> Your courage shines
> Much brighter than most
>
> To be truly brave
> Is to know how to suffer
> Hardship and sorrow
> But not grow rougher
>
> To be truly brave
> Is to keep on trying
> Even when the light
> Seems close to dying.

The music begins

Bethjain closes the book. He stands up and leaves mysteriously to the accompanying music

Somebody What was all that about? Load of ...
Some one No, wait! I wonder ...
Somebody You're as mysterious as he was.
Some one Didn't you listen to what he said?
Somebody Yes, but ...
Some one He was talking to us. It was a riddle. For us to solve.
Somebody Like a clue?
Some one Exactly! He was telling us we've been doing this whole mission wrong, Somebody. We looked up high for heroes and we should have looked low. Now do you understand?
Somebody Er ... no.
Some one We've been talking to the wrong sort of people.
Somebody (*still confused*) Oh. I see.
Some one Jack!
Somebody Where?
Some one On the telly! That was him! Nick Bethjain!
Somebody I thought he was familiar.
Some one (*moving off*) Come on, Somebody. Remember what he said: "Keep on trying—even when the light seems close to dying".

They exit. Black-out

Scene 9

During the Black-out the dustbin is brought on again

Scene 10

Back At Jack's Bin

It is almost sunset

A young boy enters secretively, searching for food

Boy O masters of the universe! I, Yardoz, lord of Kal, summon your assistance. Send us food. I am your faithful servant! (*He searches in the bin*)

Two Girls—his two elder sisters—enter and look at him

1st Girl Found anything?
Boy Not even a potato peeling. Nothing.
2nd Girl I'm starving. There must be some grub somewhere.
Boy Well, I can't find any.
2nd Girl If you didn't spend so much time pretending to be a superhero you might be more lucky.
Boy Silence! Or I'll send an army of evil Orcs to tear at your flesh! (*He moves away and changes his tone*) Anyway, if you're so clever, you find some food. (*He sits and takes out a fantasy comic to read*)
2nd Girl I can't, can I? 'Cos there isn't any left, is there? 'Cos others got here first.
1st Girl Pack it in, both of you. Strangers coming!

Automatically they run together and form a statue, depicting a poor, starving family

Some one and Somebody enter

Some one It's getting dark. But this looks like the area we started from.
Boy Oh, strangers of the afternoon, stop! We desire food!
2nd Girl Please, please, we haven't eaten for days.
1st Girl Spare us a morsel! (*They advance on them*)
Somebody Keep your distance!
Some one We haven't got anything. I'm sorry.
Somebody As a matter of fact, we're hungry ourselves.
Boy You lie, monster of the purple sky.
Some one We've nothing, honestly!
1st Girl (*to her brother and sister*) Leave off, you two. They look worse off than us.
Some one Who are you?
1st Girl Just kids.
Boy Last of the ancient lineage of Kal.
2nd Girl Scavvies. Like everyone else on the streets.

Unseen, the children's mother, Mrs Jones, enters, carrying a bag

Mrs Jones They're my children, that's who they are.

Boy (*moving to her*) You are returned. Oh, Queen Mother of Kal!
Mrs Jones That's right, son. (*To Some one and Somebody*) And who might you two be?
Somebody Just two travellers on a mission.
Mrs Jones Oh, vagrants like us, eh?
Some one More or less.
Mrs Jones Thought you were snoops from the Social for a minute — trying to take my children away from me again.
Somebody No, we don't want them, thanks.
Mrs Jones (*sitting*) Good news, kids. Look what your clever old mum's got for you. (*She opens a bag and takes some bread out*)
2nd Girl Bread! Great!
1st Girl Well done, Mum.
Boy Oh genius of the underworld.
Mrs Jones Sit down, kids, and we'll get tucked in.

The children sit around Mrs Jones

We could do with a fire. Evening's drawing in.
1st Girl There's no wood about. We looked.
2nd Girl Not even an old crate.
Mrs Jones (*to Some one and Somebody who are still standing*) Well, what are you two standing gawping at?
2nd Girl Yeah, clear off! There's nothing here for you.
Mrs Jones (*to 2nd Girl*) No need for that kind of talk! (*To Some one and Somebody*) You hungry too are you?
Somebody Well, since you ask ...
Some one We're all right.
Mrs Jones 'Course you're hungry, I can see it in your empty faces. Come over here and sit down. There's enough bread for us all.
2nd Girl Mum! I want it!
Mrs Jones Shut up! You'll get your share.
1st Girl We could save some for tomorrow, mum.
Mrs Jones I've offered them some bread and that's that! (*To Some one and Somebody*) Now stop standing around like a pair of shy squirrels, you two. Sit down!

Some one and Somebody sit near them

(*Giving some bread to them*) Here. Enjoy it before it gets stale.
Boy (*eating*) Nectar of the gods!
Some one Thank you, Mrs ... ?
Mrs Jones Jones, Mrs Jones. Mother of three. Wife of faithless Mr Jones.
Some one How come you're vagrants?
Mrs Jones That's a bit of a story. I can tell you if you like. If you've time.
Somebody Well, I'm afraid we ...
Some one Yes, please. We'd like to hear it.
Mrs Jones (*with some enthusiasm*) Well, then, I'd better start with my dear husband, Mr Roger Jones. He started us off down the slippery slope.

Scene 10

About six months ago, it must be. I remember, he came home late one Tuesday, even later than usual.

The Lights change

Mr Jones and his Girlfriend appear, as part of a flashback sequence that continues throughout Mrs Jones' story

Mr Jones Mary ... I've got something to tell you. It's like this ...
Girlfriend He's leaving you.
Mrs Jones Couldn't even tell me himself.
Girlfriend He's moving in with me.
Mrs Jones "Oh I see," I said.
1st Girl Why did Dad leave, Mum?
Mrs Jones Fancied a change of scenery, I suppose, love.
Mr Jones I'll see you're all right, Mary. Send you money for the kids each week.
Mrs Jones But he never did.
Girlfriend Time we went, Roge. Taxi's waiting.

They exit

Mrs Jones And off they went, leaving me with the kids. Never saw him again. Anyway, I had to work overtime after that — serving out the school meals to the little kiddies. We managed all right, until ...

Catering Manageress enters

Catering Manageress I'm sorry, Mrs Jones, but we've been ordered to cut back, see.
Mrs Jones "Oh, I see," I said.
Some one What happened?
Catering Manageress We'll give you a month's notice, of course.
Mrs Jones Of course. So there I was out of a job.

Catering Manageress exits

I went down to the local Job Centre to try and find another one.

Employment Officer enters

Employment Officer I'm sorry, Mrs Jones. We've no jobs available at the Centre this week. Come back next week.
Mrs Jones So back I went the next week.
Employment Officer Sorry. Try next week.
Mrs Jones And the next.
Employment Officer Maybe next week.

Employment Officer exits

Mrs Jones Nothing came up, so I stopped going down. We began to run a bit short of money. I found out that life is full of problems.
2nd Girl Mum, why can't I have a new skirt?
1st Girl Why can't I go down the disco, Mum?

Boy When's Daddy coming back, Mum?

Landlady enters

Landlady Why haven't you paid your rent, Mrs Jones?
Mrs Jones The landlady got a bit upset.
Landlady It's two months now. Two months overdue.
Mrs Jones I used to pretend I wasn't in when she knocked on the door.
Landlady I know you're in there, Mrs Jones. It's no use. I'm a very patient woman. You can't say I haven't been patient. But two months is two months, Mrs Jones. Are you listening? It's not fair, Mrs Jones. You'll have to go. By the end of the month. I mean, you must see my point of view.
Mrs Jones "Oh I see," I said. So off we went round the Council to try and get them to give us a place to live.

Council Official enters

Council Official I'm afraid there's a very long waiting list, Mrs Jones.
Mrs Jones "But where are we supposed to live?" I said.
Council Official What about your mother's house? She has several spare rooms, according to our records.

Mother enters

Mother No room at my place, dear. You go and find that husband of yours. You married him, after all. It's his responsibility.
Mrs Jones So back I went to the Council. "My mother doesn't want us", I said. She doesn't like kids.
Council Official But technically speaking she does have suitable accommodation. I am sorry. We'll put you on our list. Meanwhile, try your mother again.
Mother Try that blooming husband of yours.

Mother and Council Official exit

Mrs Jones So that was it. We were out on the streets. Surviving as best we could. Social want to put my kids in care — but I won't let them. And that's about it. Some story! Look — it's sent my kids to sleep.

Pause. Suddenly, Some one stands up

Some one Mrs Jones! I think you're the person we've been looking for!
Mrs Jones Pardon?
Somebody (*also standing up*) Yes! You're right! She shared her last bit of food with us.
Some one In spite of everything that's happened to you!
Mrs Jones What are you on about?
Somebody You haven't give up the struggle.
Some one In a cruel world, you're kind.

We hear a police siren

Scene 10

Some one ⎫ (*together*) You are the hero we've been seeking!
Somebody ⎭
Mrs Jones Me? You must be joking! If you knew the half of it!
Some one You must come with us to meet Jack.
Mrs Jones I'm no hero. Just one of thousands. Nothing special. Just an ordinary woman. Mrs Jones and her three kids.
Somebody But you're good.
Mrs Jones I'm afraid not, love. Not good. Where do you think I got this bread from?

We hear a police whistle

1st Police Officer (*off*) There she is! With all them kids!

Two Police Officers enter

2nd Police Officer Don't move, Missus. You're under arrest.
1st Police Officer For shop lifting. Get her, Nick!
Mrs Jones You'll have to catch me first, coppers. Come on kids.

They run off

Some one (*blocking the Police Officers way*) You can't arrest her! She's a hero!
1st Police Officer She's a villain. A thief and worse, probably! We've been after her for weeks. Now move out the way!

The Police Officers force past Some one and Somebody and exit

Somebody But she has to come with us to see Jack!

We hear a police siren. Pause

Mrs Jones and her children enter

Mrs Jones Have we lost them? Let's go this way. (*To Some one and Somebody*) You two still here? I should clear off if I were you—or they'll arrest you for helping me. Listen—you got it all wrong, loves. There's no such thing as heroes. Just survivors.
1st Girl Come on, Mum! They'll catch you.

The children exit

Mrs Jones All right. They haven't got me yet!

She follows

Some one I hope she doesn't get arrested.
Somebody Me too.

Pause. The Light grows darker

Some one Do you realize where we are?
Somebody Back where we started.
Some one Yes. Jack's bin. With no heroes.
Somebody And it's sunset.

Some one Do you think he's in there? (*She points to the bin*)
Somebody I don't know.
Some one Who's going to tell him?

Somebody instinctively walks up to the bin. Then he stops and comes back

Somebody You can.

Some one walks up to the bin

Some one Jack! We looked. We've been a long way. But we didn't find any heroes.
Somebody Except for Mrs Jones. And she said she wasn't either.
Some one But she was kind, Jack.
Somebody She was kind. And she's gone.
Some one Jack! Where are you?

They look in the bin. It is empty

Somebody Nothing! Empty. Just the stink of old rubbish.
Some one And yesterday's newspapers that are already out of date.
Somebody I knew he wouldn't be here.
Some one We're too late. It's dark.
Somebody He might have waited. For us to tell him.
Some one Yes. Never mind.
Somebody I mind! He was a rotten devil! He was conning us all along! (*He kicks the bin several times*)
Some one It doesn't matter. You're still Somebody. And I'm still Some one. We both know that now. Let's go.
Somebody Where to? Not to look for more heroes?
Some one No. We don't need them.
Somebody Who do we need then?
Some one You. Me. And Mrs Jones.
Somebody And her kids?
Some one Them too.
Somebody What about Jack?
Some one No. Not Jack. No one's going to rescue us.
Somebody Nobody's going to save us.
Some one But we'll survive, if we stick together.
Somebody Yes.

They move forward, then freeze

Black-out

FURNITURE AND PROPERTY LIST

Scene 1

On stage: Dustbin, covered and overflowing with rubbish
Personal: **Nobody:** mask
No one: mask

Scene 2

Strike: Dustbin
Personal: **Zap:** razor
Pow: razor
Crunch: razor
Lena: trolley

Scene 3

No props

Scene 4

On stage: Central block
Personal: **The Booties:** identical robes, silver pendant shaped like a boot
Leader: large, silver boot, mounted on a cushion
Some one: purse

Scene 5

No props

Scene 6

Personal: **Bouncer:** large bill-board advertising the concert by "The Heroes"
Fans: ticket each

Scene 7

On stage: Raised Rostrum

Scene 8

Personal: **Photographers:** cameras, photographic equipment
Some one: The Boot

SCENE 9

Off stage: Trolley **Presenter)**

Personal: **Actors:** Large blue blanket
Lancelot: horse, sword
3rd Presenter: soft toy (lion)
2nd Hoodlum: mask
1st Hoodlum: mask
Itchy: gun
Crutch: gun
Nick Bethjain: large book

SCENE 10

On stage: Dustbin

Personal: **Boy:** comic
Mrs Jones: bag. *In it:* bread

LIGHTING PLOT

Property fittings required: nil
Various simple settings—interior and exterior

To open: Spotlight on the dusbin

Cue 1	As the music stops *Lights up*	(Page 1)
Cue 2	As **Some one** exits *Black-out*	(Page 3)
Cue 3	As Scene 2 opens *Full general lighting*	(Page 3)
Cue 4	As **Lenny** and **Lena** exit *Black-out*	(Page 7)
Cue 5	As Scene 3 opens *Full general lighting*	(Page 8)
Cue 6	As **Somebody** exits *Black-out*	(Page 10)
Cue 7	As Scene 4 opens *Full general lighting*	(Page 10)
Cue 8	As **The Booties** exit *Black-out*	(Page 13)
Cue 9	As Scene 5 opens *Full general lighting*	(Page 13)
Cue 10	As **Somebody** and **Some one** exit *Black-out*	(Page 14)
Cue 11	As Scene 6 opens *Full general lighting*	(Page 14)
Cue 12	As **Somebody** and **Some one** exit *Black-out*	(Page 15)
Cue 13	As Scene 7 opens *Lights up on the Announcer*	(Page 15)
Cue 14	As the chorus finishes *Black-out*	(Page 17)
Cue 15	As Scene 8 opens *Full general lighting*	(Page 18)

Cue 16	As **Some one** exits *Black-out*	(Page 20)
Cue 17	As Scene 9 opens *Dim lighting only*	(Page 20)
Cue 18	As **Guinevere** enters *Lights up on the "screen"*	(Page 21)
Cue 19	As **Some one** and **Somebody** exit *Black-out*	(Page 26)
Cue 20	As Scene 10 opens *Sunset effect*	(Page 27)
Cue 21	**Mrs Jones:** "... even later than usual." *General interior lighting*	(Page 29)
Cue 22	**Somebody:** "Me too." *Lights dim*	(Page 31)
Cue 23	As **Some one** and **Somebody** freeze *Black-out*	(Page 32)

EFFECTS PLOT

Cue 1	To open *Eerie music*	(Page 1)
Cue 2	As **Lena** and **Lenny** exit *Music*	(Page 7)
Cue 3	At end of Scene 7 *Music*	(Page 17)
Cue 4	Immediately after **Somebody** throws the Boot off *Sound of crashing glass*	(Page 20)
Cue 5	As Scene 9 opens *Noise of several television channels working at once*	(Page 20)
Cue 6	As **Guinevere** enters *Music*	(Page 21)
Cue 7	**Guinevere:** "Oh darling Lancelot!" *Sound of thundering hooves*	(Page 21)
Cue 8	As the **Presenters** enter *Music*	(Page 22)
Cue 9	**2nd Presenter:** "Up you get!" *Music*	(Page 23)
Cue 10	**Voice Over:** "... of San Fernando." *Music*	(Page 24)
Cue 11	**Girl:** "... and rescue me!" *Music*	(Page 25)
Cue 12	**Hoodlums:** "... and Sergeant Crutch!" *Music*	(Page 25)
Cue 13	**Voice Over:** "... with Nick Bethjain." *Organ music*	(Page 25)
Cue 14	**Nick Bethjain:** "Seems close to dying." *Music*	(Page 26)
Cue 15	**Some one:** "In a cruel world, you're kind." *Sound of a police siren*	(Page 26)
Cue 16	**Mrs Jones:** "... I got this bread from?" *Sound of a police whistle*	(Page 31)
Cue 17	**Somebody:** "... come with us to see Jack!" *Sound of police siren*	(Page 31)

MADE AND PRINTED IN GREAT BRITAIN BY
LATIMER TREND & COMPANY LTD PLYMOUTH
MADE IN ENGLAND

www.ingramcontent.com/pod-product-compliance
Ingram Content Group UK Ltd.
Pitfield, Milton Keynes, MK11 3LW, UK
UKHW021832190526
5880IPUK00015B/138